USBORNE SUPERSKILLS
IMPROVE YOUR
RUNNING
SKILLS

Susan Peach

Running consultants:

Norman Brook
(British Amateur Athletics Board National Coach) and

Charlie Spedding
(Olympic medallist and winner of the 1984 London marathon)

Designed by **Stephen Wright**

Additional designs by **Graham Round**

Illustrated by **Paul Wilding, Paul Sullivan, Steve Cross** and **Chris Lyon**

Photographs by **David Cannon (All-Sport UK)**

Models: **Andrea Forster, Richard Hunter** and **Cathy Muscat**

Cover designed by **Chris Scollen** and illustrated by **Gordon Lawson**

This book was produced in association with **UK.**

Contents

First published in 1988 by Usborne Publishing Ltd, 83-84 Saffron Hill, London EC1N 8RT, England. Copyright © 1994 1988 Usborne Publishing Ltd.

Printed in Belgium.

Introduction by David Moorcroft

When I was at school, running was something we did when it was too wet to play football. Fortunately times have changed. Thousands of people of all ages, sizes and abilities now take part in fun runs and races all over the country. Add to that the increasing popularity of televised athletics competitions, and it is not surprising that more and more young people are being attracted to the sport.

Not everyone can become a champion though, nor should you start by copying the training schedules of Olympic champions. For young people it is important to get the basics right, not to do too much too quickly and not to be impatient for success. Improvement is a long-term process requiring both determination and a good deal of patience.

Runners mature at different ages. Some who are world beaters at 15 never get much better, while others who plod away during their teens develop into very good runners at a later age. The very best you can ask of yourself is to fulfill your potential, whatever that may be.

No matter what level we run at, we share similar experiences: the disappointment of a bad run, the frustration of injuries and the great pleasure of a personal best.

Running is a great activity. This book is full of straightforward and sensible tips which will help you to improve as a runner, and ultimately to enjoy the sport more.

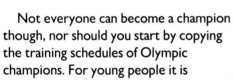

David Moorcroft

About running

Although people have always run, the first records of organized running events date from the time of the Ancient Greeks. Their young men used sport as a way to keep fit for warfare. Sporting events were also included in some of their religious festivals. The most famous of these were the Olympic Games, which took place every four years between 776BC and 393AD.

There were three running events, which took place on a flat area of ground about 192m long and 30m wide. The *stade**, which involved running one length of the ground, and the *diaulos*, which was two lengths, were both sprint races. The *dolichos*, which was 20 lengths, was a long distance race.

This picture, taken from a Greek vase, shows runners in the *stade* race.

An early hurdles race. Athletes jumped over a series of wooden gates, which were known as hurdles.

The next important stage in the development of competitive running was the holding of rural athletics meetings. These started in the Middle Ages. Many of today's events were invented at rural meetings in England and Scotland. For example, hurdling was a race which involved clearing a series of gates or fences, while steeplechase was a race between two church steeples in neighbouring villages.

In the nineteenth century there was a revival of interest in running. Contests between two runners, often known as pedestrian races, became a popular form of entertainment. Spectators often placed large bets on the outcome of the races, and many runners were able to earn their living from taking part in these events.

In 1896 a Frenchman named Baron Pierre de Coubertin organized the first modern Olympic Games. Only 59 competitors took part, but this event marked the beginning of modern international competitions.

In 1885 a famous pedestrian called W.G. George ran the mile in only 4 minutes 12.75 seconds in a race against W. Cummings.

*The word "stadium" comes from the name of this race.

In the twentieth century running performances have improved steadily, helped by technological advances such as the invention of synthetic track surfaces, better running shoes and more efficient timing equipment.

In recent years there has been a running boom. This is partly due to the televising of athletics meetings and of mass-participation runs, which has inspired people to try running. Many other people have taken up running because of the benefits it brings to their health.

Modern equipment can give split-second times.

Since the 1970s many major marathons have been televised.

How to use this book

This book is divided into several sections which cover each of the main types of running, such as sprinting or cross-country. In each section you will find a sequence of step-by-step photos, which illustrate good running technique for the particular events. Try to memorize the body positions shown, so that you can try to improve your own technique when you run.

Circular photos like these show running technique.

Each section also includes a target chart, which you can use to monitor your progress. Time yourself over the relevant distance, then see how your result compares with the target times for your age group. To be accurate, you will need to use a stop-watch, or get a friend to time you. Repeat the test over a period of a few weeks to see if you can achieve a "Gold" time.

Training technique

Throughout the book you will find a series of training techniques, which are highlighted by a yellow flash like the one above.

These are training methods used by top athletes, which you can use to improve your running and your general fitness. Each technique is explained fully and there are suggestions on how to use it in your training sessions. Before you start any of these techniques, you should do some warm-up exercises like the ones shown on pages 36-37.

You can also use this book to help you plan your training programme over a whole year. At the back of the book you will find charts compiled by a top running coach, which give comprehensive details of suitable annual training programmes for sprinters, hurdlers or longer distance runners.

All the distances in this book are given in metric measurements. If you prefer to use the imperial system, there is a conversion chart on page 43 which gives the equivalent imperial distances.

5

Jogging: getting started

Jogging is the easiest form of running to take up. You can do it anywhere and you do not have to be extremely fit to take part. On these two pages you can find out how to get started.

Before you set out

★ You can wear any loose, comfortable clothes, such as shorts and a T-shirt, or a track suit. The only essential piece of specialist equipment is a pair of proper running trainers.

★ Before each run you should go through a short warm-up exercise routine (see pages 36-37). This stretches and loosens your muscles and tendons and lessens the chance of injuring them.

★ You can run at any time of day, but always leave at least two hours between a meal and a run to avoid indigestion.

★ If possible, persuade a friend to jog with you. Having someone to talk to and encourage you will make things much easier.

Where to run

You can run on any surface, but it is a good idea to get off the road or pavement whenever possible. Your local park or playing fields are ideal places to jog, as the softer ground helps to absorb the jolt that your legs receive as your feet strike the ground.

If you do jog in the streets, stay on the pavement. If you have to jog in the road, always run on the side facing the oncoming traffic so that you can see any approaching cars. Use your common sense about where you jog. You should not jog alone in deserted areas, such as back streets, and it is always best to jog during daylight hours.

You can read more about kit on page 35.

You can read more about shoes on pages 32-34.

How often to run

Once or twice a week is about right when you first start. While you are in your teens your bones, muscles and tendons are still growing and it is possible to cause permanent damage if you do too much of any one exercise. This is particularly true of running, as the constant pounding of your feet on the ground puts a lot of stress on your feet and legs. If you want to take more exercise, try other activities such as cycling or swimming.

How far to go

Stage	Distance*	Time	Limits
1	800m	5 mins	11 year olds should stop at stage 3
2	1,200m	7 mins	
3	1,600m	9 mins	
4	2,000m	11 mins	12 year olds should stop at stage 6
5	2,400m	13 mins	
6	2,800m	15 mins	
7	3,200m	17 mins	13 year olds should stop at stage 9
8	3,600m	19 mins	
9	4,000m	21 mins	
10	4,400m	23 mins	14 year olds and over
11	4,800m	25 mins	

The training programme above will help you to start jogging and then build up your distance. You can either jog for the recommended distance or for the length of time, whichever is easier to work out. Start at stage one and take it very slowly. If you get out of breath, you probably started out too fast, so slow down or walk for a bit to recover. When you start jogging again, go slower. Repeat this run once or twice a week until you can manage it easily, then move on to the next stage. Stick to the targets for your age-group, as running further could lead to injuries.

Jogging technique

You should jog at a very slow and relaxed pace so that you do not get breathless. It should be possible to hold a conversation as you jog.

Arms loosely bent

Low knee lift

Short stride

Hands cupped

Take shortish strides and don't raise your knees up high. Your arms should be slightly bent and should swing loosely at your sides. Try not to swing your arms across your chest or clench your fists as this will make you very tense.

Warming down

The tips below will help you to warm down after your run. You will need to do this to avoid stiffness the next day (see right).

★ As you reach the end of your jog, don't sprint for home. Slow down instead.
★ Do some exercises to help your muscles cool down slowly (see pages 36-37).
★ As soon as you stop exercising, put on some warm clothes, such as a track suit.
★ It is a good idea to have a warm bath or shower after exercising.

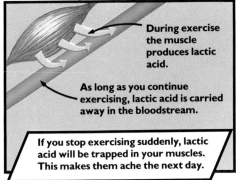

During exercise the muscle produces lactic acid.

As long as you continue exercising, lactic acid is carried away in the bloodstream.

If you stop exercising suddenly, lactic acid will be trapped in your muscles. This makes them ache the next day.

You can find the equivalent imperial distances on page 43.

Jogging: taking part in a race

Once you have mastered the basics of jogging you may want to test out your new-found skills in a fun run or race. Below you can read lots of tips for taking part in these events, as well as finding out about some useful training techniques to speed you on your way.

Coping with hills

Training technique

When you approach a hill, change your jogging technique as shown on the right. Even experienced runners can be winded by hills, so it is a good idea to set aside a training session every few weeks to work on your hill technique. Practise by running to the brow of the hill then jogging slowly down to recover.

Lean forwards into the hill.

Slow down.

Look straight ahead, not upwards at the brow of the hill.

Take shorter strides.

Taking part in a fun run

Once you get used to jogging, you may like to take part in an organized run. The best kind to start off with is a fun run, which is a non-competitive event. You can find out about fun runs in your area through your local newspaper or through specialized running magazines.

There are usually no age restrictions on how far you can run in a fun run. However, if you run too far you can injure yourself (see page 6), so it is best not to go further than the recommended distances shown in the chart on the right.

Age	Distance
11	3,000m
12	4,000m
13	5,000m
14	6,500m
15+	10,000m

Fun run tips

★ Don't start off at top speed – you will end up exhausted half-way through the course. It is better to keep to a steady pace all the way. Remember this is not a race – everyone who crosses the finishing line is a winner.

★ You will lose a lot of fluid through sweat, so you should replace as much as possible immediately after the race. There may be drinks provided at the finish, or you could take your own with you to the run. Glucose drinks provide a good source of energy that can be quickly digested.

★ If you are injured or in pain, stop straight away and report for first aid. If you carry on you will make the injury worse.

Runners of all ages and abilities can take part in a fun run.

Road racing

Many people who start out jogging go on to take part in road races. These are competitive events which take place on roads and paths.

There are strict age restrictions on the distances teenagers are allowed to run in these races. For example, you are not allowed to take part in a marathon (26.2 miles/42,195m) until you are over 18. However, there are many shorter distance races that teenagers are allowed to enter, such as 5,000m or 10,000m.

Although road racing is basically the same style of running as jogging, it is usually done at a much faster pace. It is therefore a good idea to include some speed work in your training. You could try some of the techniques used by cross-country and track runners, such as interval training (see page 16) or fartlek (see page 11), or you could use the method shown here.

Increasing your speed

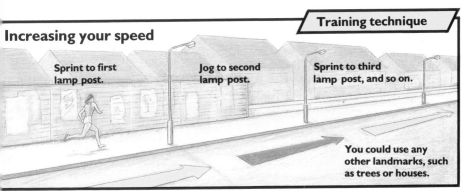

Training technique

Sprint to first lamp post.

Jog to second lamp post.

Sprint to third lamp post, and so on.

You could use any other landmarks, such as trees or houses.

Joining a club

A good incentive to help you keep up and improve your jogging is to join a local running club. These are usually run on a very informal basis with members meeting up once or twice a week to go jogging in a group. They are usually delighted to recruit new members, so don't feel intimidated about joining.

The advantages of a club are that you always have someone to go jogging with, there are plenty of people to advise and encourage you, and it is a good chance to make new friends.

Keeping a running diary

Once you start jogging (or any other type of running) on a regular basis, it is a good idea to keep a diary. This helps you to measure your progress.

If you are taking part in races, your diary can be a useful record of how successful your preparation was.

Things you should record in your diary are listed on the right.

A stop-watch (see page 35) will help you to keep an accurate record of your runs.

★ How far you ran.
★ How long it took you.
★ Where you ran. Was it in the park or on the pavement? Were there lots of hills?
★ What the weather was like. If it was very hot, very windy or icy this may have slowed you down.
★ How you felt. Were you exhausted or did you manage the run easily?

MON Uphill Run (25 mins)

TUES

THURS

FRI

SAT 3km Fun r

SUN

...for ...mins.

Cross-country: preparation and training

Cross-country running usually takes place in a large park or in the countryside. Most of the course is grass, but it could also include tracks or even ploughed fields. Runners may have to negotiate natural barriers such as gates, walls or ditches, as well as muddy ground and several uphill and downhill stretches.*

These difficult conditions mean that cross-country running requires a high level of strength and stamina. You can read about how to prepare and train for this strenuous event on these two pages.

Cross-country clothing

Cross-country events are normally held in winter. In fact many track athletes use cross-country as a way to keep fit out of season. As this is a winter sport, it is important to be prepared for cold or wet weather.

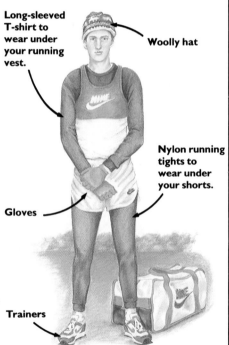

Long-sleeved T-shirt to wear under your running vest.

Woolly hat

Nylon running tights to wear under your shorts.

Gloves

Trainers

In addition to your basic kit (see page 35), you should wear some extra warm clothing, as shown above. The best shoes for cross-country conditions are spiked running shoes or trainers with good sole grips (see page 33). Remember also to take some dry clothing to change into after the race.

Warming up

You must warm up before a cross-country run as it is easy to pull a muscle or tendon in these cold conditions. Keep your track suit or other warm clothes on while you warm up.

Stand with your feet apart. Hold your arms as shown on the left. Stretch as far as you can to one side. Repeat on the other side.

Hold your foot with one hand. Pull your heel away from your bottom to stretch the front of your leg. Repeat with the other leg.

Keeping your legs straight, bend down and clasp one ankle. Push your head towards your hands. Repeat with the other leg.

You should begin your warm-up routine at least 20 minutes before your run. Start off with some gentle jogging for about five minutes. Follow this with ten minutes of stretching exercises like the ones shown above. Then do six runs of 50-60m gradually increasing your speed each run.

*In some countries courses are artificially constructed on horse racing tracks, using straw bales as obstacles.

Hill running

Swing your arms.

High knee lift

This is an exercise which uses hills to build up your leg muscles and increase your overall strength. It is an exaggerated style which you should not use to tackle hills on your normal runs*. Practise on a fairly steep hill, about 60-150m in length. Sprint up the hill, pushing hard against the ground and lifting your knees high. Swing your arms backwards and forwards to balance the leg action. Walk back down the hill to recover. Repeat this several times.

Fartlek

Fartlek is a Swedish word meaning "speed play". It is a type of cross-country running used for training in which you run fast and slow stretches according to the kind of terrain and how you feel. Part of a typical fartlek run is shown below.

Sprint on flat ground.

Run hard uphill.

Jog to recover.

Jog down to recover.

As the pictures show, fartlek should include a variety of paces from sprinting to slow jogging. Use the jogs to recover from the fast or difficult stretches, but speed up the pace again as soon as possible. As you improve, you should increase the number of difficult stretches and reduce the jogging time.

If possible, run your first few sessions with a more experienced runner. Once you have got the hang of it, though, it is an easy technique to practise on your own in the local park. Fartlek is used by track athletes as well as cross-country runners as the variety of terrain and speed makes it an interesting form of training.

Cross-country targets (times in minutes)

Age	Distance	Gold Boys / Girls	Silver Boys / Girls	Bronze Boys / Girls
11	1500m	5:25 / 5:45	6:30 / 7:10	7:50 / 9:00
12	1500m	5:15 / 5:40	6:10 / 7:00	7.30 / 8:50
13	2000m	7:00 / 7:30	8:10 / 9:30	10:00 / 11:30
14	2000m	6:45 / 7:15	7:55 / 9:15	9:40 / 11:20
15	3000m	10:20 / 11:25	12:00 / 13:20	13:30 / 15:30
16+	3000m	10:00 / 11:05	11:30 / 13:00	13:00 / 15:00

*During a run, use the hill technique shown on page 8.

Cross-country: race tactics

If you enjoy cross-country running, sooner or later you may want to enter a race to test yourself against other runners. On these two pages you will find some race-winning tactics* as well as useful tips for coping with difficult cross-country conditions.

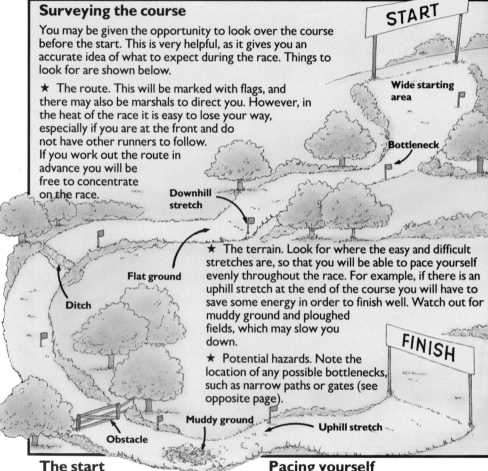

Surveying the course

You may be given the opportunity to look over the course before the start. This is very helpful, as it gives you an accurate idea of what to expect during the race. Things to look for are shown below.

★ The route. This will be marked with flags, and there may also be marshals to direct you. However, in the heat of the race it is easy to lose your way, especially if you are at the front and do not have other runners to follow. If you work out the route in advance you will be free to concentrate on the race.

START

Wide starting area

Bottleneck

Downhill stretch

Flat ground

Ditch

★ The terrain. Look for where the easy and difficult stretches are, so that you will be able to pace yourself evenly throughout the race. For example, if there is an uphill stretch at the end of the course you will have to save some energy in order to finish well. Watch out for muddy ground and ploughed fields, which may slow you down.

★ Potential hazards. Note the location of any possible bottlenecks, such as narrow paths or gates (see opposite page).

FINISH

Muddy ground

Obstacle

Uphill stretch

The start

There is usually a wide starting area to avoid early bunching of the runners. It is important to get off to a good start, as the course is likely to narrow after a few hundred metres, making it difficult to pass. The first 200-300m of a course are usually taken at a very fast pace, as runners attempt to get ahead of the pack. Try to keep up with the leaders at this stage.

Pacing yourself

If you have been able to survey the course, you will have a good idea of what obstacles lie ahead. You must pace yourself so that you will have enough energy to manage the entire course. Do not continue the fast starting pace for any longer than is necessary, otherwise you will tire early in the race. Try to relax into your coasting pace as soon as possible.

 *There is more information about entering a race on pages 44-45.

Bottlenecks

here is a limit to the number of runners who can get over a gate or through a narrow part of the course at once. If you re caught in a large group at these obstacles you will waste valuable time waiting to get through. If possible, speed up to get ahead of the group as you approach a potential bottleneck.

Downhill stretches

If necessary, use your arms to help you keep your balance.

ry to avoid getting caught in a group f runners on a downhill stretch. If it is ippery, another runner may fall in ront of you, or if you are jostled, you ay fall yourself. Try to get out of the ack so that you have a clear downhill un.

On a downhill stretch allow the lope to carry you along. Lengthen and uicken your stride and keep your ody fairly upright. As long as you stay elaxed it will be possible to run very ast.

Do not try to check your stride length.

Obstacles

You will usually have to get over an obstacle, such as a wall or a gate. You can climb over (see left) or vault it (see right), according to the height and how much energy you have.

Wet or muddy ground

ry to get over this as quickly as ossible. Make sure your shoe-laces are ecurely tied, as it is very easy to lose hoes in the mud.

The finish

t is normal race practice to sprint the inal stretch to the finish line. This is artly to throw off any close rivals and artly to improve your time over the ourse. You should start your final print about 60-100m from the finish ine. Never start to sprint until you are vithin sight of the finish.

After the race

When you have finished the course, be sure to report to one of the officials. In big races there may be a marshal to take note of your number and your finishing time as you complete the race. This is to check that all the runners have returned safely. If you do not check in, they may assume that you are lost or injured and send out a search party to look for you.

Remember to put on your track suit as soon as you finish the race. You may feel warm, but cooling down too quickly will make you ache the next day (see page 7).

Middle distance: technique

Races which are run on a track are normally divided into sprinting, middle distance and long distance events. The term "middle distance" is used to refer to the 800m and 1500m races. The mile is also considered to be a middle distance event, although it is not run at all competitions.

On the right you can read about how your body produces the energy required for middle distance running. Below you can find out about correct running technique and how to achieve it.

How your body produces energy

As you run, your muscles contract and relax to move your arms and legs. To do this, they need energy, which comes from the food you eat. There are two methods which your body can use to convert food into energy. The first method uses oxygen and is called aerobic. The second does not use oxygen and is called anaerobic.

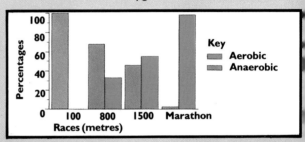

Key
■ Aerobic
■ Anaerobic

The chart above shows what percentages of the energy required for different races are provided by the two systems. The aerobic system can provide lots of energy, but it provides it slowly. The longer an event lasts, the more energy comes from the aerobic process. The anaerobic system provides a limited amount of energy very quickly, and is most important in short events, like sprints.

Middle distance runners run too fast for the aerobic system alone, and too long for the anaerobic system alone. They therefore get their energy from both systems simultaneously.

Middle distance technique

Reach out with your lower leg and land on the ball of your right foot. Your feet and knees should point straight ahead at all times, ensuring that your drive is in a forward direction, not wasted to the left or right.

As your right foot begins to push off, bend your left leg and swing it forwards. Your arms should be flexed at about 90° and should swing backwards and forwards, slightly across your body. Keep your hands loosely cupped.

Running out of oxygen

During intense exercise, you may require more oxygen than you can take in. This is known as oxygen debt. Lactic acid (a waste product of the anaerobic system) starts to build up in your muscles, making your legs and arms feel heavy and difficult to move.

Middle distance runners are most prone to lactic acid build-up, because they run for long periods at a pace which requires more oxygen than they can take in.

Middle distance training

Through training (see pages 16-17), you can improve your body's efficiency in two important ways: by increasing the amount of oxygen that you can take in, (often referred to as your maximum oxygen uptake or VO_2max), and by increasing the amount of lactic acid that you can tolerate. These two things help you to run faster, and to keep going for longer, both of which are vital in middle distance races.

Rear leg extended

Front leg extended

At the push-off, your right leg should be fully extended behind you. Your left leg should be picked up high, ready to take the next stride. Your head and shoulders should be steady and relaxed, and should point straight forwards at all times.

Running drills

The drills below will help to improve your running action. For each exercise, run about 60m, concentrating on a single aspect of your style.

1 Elbows

As you run, swing your elbows back and up without raising your shoulders. Keep your elbows close to your sides.

2 Shoulders

Shrug your shoulders up to your ears, then push them down. Run with them in this low position.

3 Rear extension*

As you push off, extend your leg behind you. Keep your foot in contact with the ground for as long as possible.

4 Knees

Pick up your knees as you run. Try to keep your body in an upright position – do not lean forwards or backwards.

5 Front extension*

As you stride forwards, reach out with your lower leg and then pull your foot back to strike the ground.

*Good hip mobility is vital for this movement. There are exercises to improve this on pages 36-37.

Middle distance: training

Many different training techniques are used for middle distance. They divide up into three groups: aerobic endurance exercises, which increase maximum oxgygen uptake*; anaerobic exercises, which increase lactic acid tolerance*; and speed exercises.

Aerobic training techniques

Continuous slow running

Continuous running, can be done anywhere and is a good break from training on a track. Continuous running will increase your stamina and strength.

The aim is to run at a pace which keeps a balance between the amount of oxygen you take in and the amount you are using, which is why this is sometimes known as "steady state" running. The pace should take your pulse (see page 38) to around 170 beats per minute. As a rough guide, 11-14 year olds should run for up to 20 minutes, while anyone over 15 should run for up to 45 minutes.

Interval training

This consists of running fast over a set distance, followed by a slow jog or a timed rest before the next effort. A typical training session which you could try is shown in the diagram on the right. The main benefit of interval training is to improve your oxygen uptake, but it also increases your basic speed.

As you improve, you will need to make the session more difficult in order to gain the same benefit. This can be done in several ways: by increasing the distance you run, by reducing the amount of recovery time, or by increasing the number of repetitions.

You should take your pulse rate several times during the training session to check

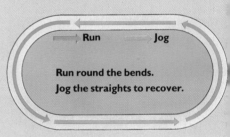

Run   Jog

Run round the bends.
Jog the straights to recover.

Repeat these fast and slow sections without stopping. Start with 6-8 laps of the track.

that you are exercising at about the right intensity. Your pulse should be around 180-185 beats per minute after a fast effort and 120-130 beats per minute after a recovery jog.

Your heart and exercise

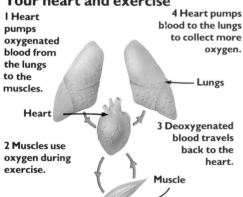

I Heart pumps oxygenated blood from the lungs to the muscles.

Heart

2 Muscles use oxygen during exercise.

3 Deoxygenated blood travels back to the heart.

4 Heart pumps blood to the lungs to collect more oxygen.

Lungs

Muscle

Like other muscles, your heart gets stronger if you exercise regularly. The stronger it becomes, the more blood it can pump through with each beat.

If you repeat the same exercise regularly over a few weeks, it will start to feel easier. This is because your heart can carry the necessary amount of blood to your muscles with fewer beats. Taking your pulse (see page 38) is therefore a good way to measure how much you have improved.

* See pages 14-15.

Resistance training

Hill running, running on sand or snow, or in shallow water are all forms of resistance training. This technique uses difficult running conditions to increase your leg strength and your anaerobic endurance.

A session of resistance training on soft, loose sand might consist of running for 20-30 seconds, followed by a long enough break for your pulse to return to 120-130 beats. Repeat this three times, have a long break to recover, then try the whole session again to see if you can improve.

Swing your arms in an exaggerated fashion.

Lift your knees up high.

Use long strides.

Repetition running

This is a variation of interval training, but instead of increasing your oxygen uptake, the session is structured to improve your tolerance of lactic acid. This is done by running for short distances at a fast pace and then reducing the recovery period, which may consist of rest or walking instead of jogging.

The most important factor is the speed. You should aim to run the fast stretches at your racing pace, or even faster.

Try these sessions:
★ 2 sets of 4 x 150m, walking round the rest of the track to recover, with a 15 minute recovery between sets.
★ 1 set of 4 x 300m with 3-5 minute recovery periods.

Middle distance races are usually run at a fast pace, with a sprint at the end. You will therefore need to devote some of your training to improving your speed. The techniques in the sprinting section (see pages 22-23) will all be helpful.

For middle distance purposes, it is a good idea to practise sprinting towards the end of your training session, when you are tired. This develops your ability to accelerate to a sprint under race conditions.

Speed is vital at the end of a middle distance race.

In a close finish, the ability to sprint for the line may win you the race.

Middle distance: race tactics

Both the 800m and the 1500m are track races. The 800m starts on a bend and takes two complete laps of the track*, whereas the 1500m starts on a straight and takes three and three-quarter laps. Success in both these races depends on good tactics.

The start

All track races of 800m or more use a standing start, which is shown below. The starter will give you two commands: "On your marks" and then the starting gun. Follow these instructions to get off to a successful start.

On your marks...

Stand with one foot just behind the starting line and the other foot about 30cm behind. One arm should be forwards with the other arm back.

Go!

Push off hard from your front leg and bring your back leg forwards to take the first step. Swing your arms as shown above to help your starting thrust.

Runner enters the inside lane here.

Runner can leave lane here.

Runner drawn in lane 8.

Start

In the 800m, you must stay in your lane for the first 100m. The point at which you may leave your lane is marked by red flags and a green line on the track. Once past the green line, you should try to get into the inside lane (lane 1), as this allows you to run the shortest distance.

If you are drawn in one of the outside lanes, do not rush to the inside of the track as soon as you pass the line. Instead follow the shorter route shown in the diagram on the left, and be careful not to collide with other runners on the way.

The 1500m is not run in lanes, and runners are free to break for the inside lane from the start.

Getting into a good position

It is important to be among the leaders early in the race, as it can be difficult to catch up later, particularly if you are caught in a pack of runners.

However, it is not always a good idea to be the leader, as this runner is responsible for setting the pace, which puts him under a lot of psychological pressure. The leader also has to cope with full air-resistance, whereas for a runner who tucks in behind him this can be reduced by up to 64% (see diagram).

The ideal position is to be about one metre behind the leader. From here you can keep contact with the leader, and you will also be able to react to any moves made by runners coming from behind.

Leader has to push through full air-resistance.

Air stream

Runner about one metre behind, matching him stride for stride, faces much less air-resistance. This is often referred to as slip-streaming.

* One lap in the inside lane of a standard track measures 400m.

Getting boxed in

You should be careful not to get boxed in. This is when you find yourself surrounded by other runners and are unable to control your own pace. Most cases of boxing-in occur in the pack. The best way to avoid the problem is to get into position behind the leader, where you will not be so much at risk.

If you do get boxed in, there are two things you can do: either drop back and then go round the outside of the pack, or maintain the pace and watch for a space.

Runner number 10 is boxed in by her opponents.   This runner is in an ideal position.

Passing

Normally you should pass on the outside. If you pass on the inside, make sure there is space, as if you jostle another runner you could be disqualified. Don't cut in right in front of an opponent – make sure you are one stride ahead before you move over.

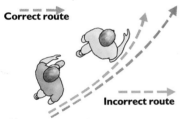

Correct route

Incorrect route

Always pass with conviction, otherwise your opponent may let you tow him along for a while before passing you again.

The final lap

The start of the final lap is signalled by a bell. The last part of a middle distance race is usually taken at a very fast pace. This is often called the final kick. Most runners start their kick with about 100-200m to go and, if it is a very close race, the last few metres can turn into a sprint for the finish line.

Runners who are not powerful sprinters often start their kick much earlier than this to give them a head start over the fast finishers. If you decide to start your kick early (say at the beginning of the final lap) make sure you can maintain the pace you set right up to the finish. It is no good starting your final effort and then slowing down half-way.

You should aim to keep running at full speed until you are a few metres past the finish line. This is because if you aim for the actual line you will unconsciously start to slow down just before you reach it. This could cost you the race.

Middle distance targets (times in minutes)

Age	800m			1500m		
	Gold	Silver	Bronze	Gold	Silver	Bronze
	Boys / Girls	Boys / Girls	Boys / Girls	Boys / Girls	Boys / Girls	Boys / Girls
11	2:30 / 2:40	2:40 / 3:00	3:10 / 3:40	5:15 / 5:35	6:00 / 6:20	6:50 / 7:25
12	2:25 / 2:35	2:35 / 2:55	2:50 / 3:30	5:00 / 5:30	5:45 / 6:15	6:30 / 7:15
13	2:15 / 2:30	2:30 / 2:50	2:45 / 3:20	4:35 / 5:20	5:20 / 6:00	6:10 / 7:00
14	2:10 / 2:25	2:25 / 2:40	2:40 / 3:10	4:25 / 5:10	5:00 / 5:55	5:45 / 6:40
15	2:05 / 2:20	2:20 / 2:35	2:35 / 3:00	4:20 / 4:50	4:50 / 5:35	5:35 / 6:20
16+	2:00 / 2:15	2:15 / 2:30	2:30 / 2:50	4:10 / 4:40	4:40 / 5:20	5:20 / 6:00

Long distance track events

There are three long distance track races: 3,000m (7.5 laps of the track), 5,000m (12.5 laps) and 10,000m (25 laps). At junior meetings some shorter distances, such as 2,000m, are also run because of age restrictions on the longer distances. Technique and training for these races are similar to middle distance (see pages 14-19), but long distance races are particularly suited to runners with lots of stamina.

Training for long distance

★ Long distance races are run at a fairly steady pace, so most of the energy you need is provided aerobically (see pages 14-15). Your training should therefore consist mainly of aerobic techniques, such as continuous running and interval training (see page 16).

★ Do not neglect speed work (see pages 22-23), as you will need to be able to cope with changes of pace and a sprint finish.

★ Many long distance runners use cross-country running (see pages 10-13) as part of their training. It requires great stamina and therefore improves your ability to cope with long track races.

Interval training for long distance

| 1 | 8 x 200m with 90 second recovery jogs. |

| 2 | 4 x 400m with 2 minute recovery jogs. |

Some intervals you could try for long distance are shown above. You should run the fast stretches at 75-80% of your top speed. This pace should take your pulse to a maximum of about 190 beats per minute after a fast stretch, and about 130 beats per minute after the recovery period.

Race tips

★ You do not have to keep up with the front runners from the start, as you will have plenty of time to catch up later.

★ Make sure you run the shortest distance. Keep to the inside lanes and avoid running wide, especially on the bends.

★ Slip-streaming (see page 18) is very important in long distance races. If possible, you should stay tucked in behind another runner to save energy.

★ Don't lead for long periods unless you know you can run faster than the rest of the field. The effort of running at the front is greater than in middle distance because of the extra length of the race.

★ Try to keep to an even pace for as much of the race as possible. This is much less tiring than running fast and slow stretches.

A lapped runner should move out to let a faster runner through.

Path of lapped runner

Path of faster runner

Coping with stragglers

As the race progresses, it is common for the leading runners to lap the runners at the back of the field. This can cause problems if the stragglers stay in the inside lane, forcing you to weave in and out of them.

Out of courtesy, many runners will move out into lane 2 or 3 to let you pass. If stragglers are blocking the inside lane, try shouting "Track!" to let them know that you are there. If they still don't move, you will have to move out to overtake.

Changing pace

Speeding up and then slowing down the pace is known as surging. Some runners use this tactic to throw off opponents who are not able to keep up with the faster pace. If one of your opponents surges during a race, you have to decide whether to follow or to stick to your own pace.

★ Early in a race, keep to your own pace. Unless your opponent is very strong, he will tire himself by surging and you will be able to catch up later.

★ Runners who are not good at a sprint finish may start to surge or make a long run for home with two or three laps to go. If you are a strong sprinter you can overtake them in the final lap.

★ If someone surges in the final lap, you must keep up with them. There is no time to catch up later, and if you don't keep up you will lose.

Surging — Training technique

As surging is very tiring, you should not try to do it in a race unless you have practised first in training. To build up your stamina for surging, use the technique shown below in your training sessions.

1. Run the first 200m at your normal race pace.

2. Run the next 200m at a faster pace.

3. Drop back to race pace for the final 200m.

In all you should run 3-6 sets of 600m with 2-5 minutes recovery time between sets.

How muscles work

Your muscles can contract and relax because they are made up of thousands of fibres which are capable of becoming longer or shorter. There are two types of muscle fibre, shown in the diagram below.

Slow twitch, or red muscle fibre. These are used for slow, aerobic work.

Muscle

Bundle of muscle fibres

Fast twitch, or white muscle fibre. These are used for fast, anaerobic work.

Normally muscle fibres are divided about equally between slow and fast twitch fibres. However, some people have a predominance of one type of fibre, which makes them more suited to either aerobic or anaerobic work. Runners who can keep going for long distances but cannot sprint probably have lots of slow twitch fibres and few fast twitch fibres.

Long distance targets (times in minutes)

| | 3,000m | | |
Age	Gold Boys / Girls	Silver Boys / Girls	Bronze Boys / Girls
11	11:05 / 11:40	12:40 / 13:50	15:10 / 16:00
12	10:40 / 11:30	11:55 / 13:30	14:20 / 15:45
13	10:05 / 11:15	11:20 / 12:40	13:10 / 15:22
14	9:45 / 10:55	10:55 / 12:20	12:20 / 14:50
15	9:25 / 10:25	10:30 / 11:40	11:45 / 13:50
16+	9:05 / 10:05	10:05 / 11:15	11:15 / 12:40

Sprinting: technique and training

A sprint is a short run at full speed. The term "sprint" is used to describe the three shortest races: the 100m, 200m and 400m. The 100m is run on the straight, the 200m consists of a bend and the straight, while the 400m is one complete lap of the track. All sprint races are run in lanes.

To do well in the sprint events, you need fast reactions and good technique, as shown in the photos on the right.

As you drive forward from your left foot, your right leg should swing forward with your heel tucked under your bottom. Your arms should be bent at about 90° and should pump backwards and forwards in time with your strides.

Sprinting targets (times in seconds)

100m

Age	Gold Boys / Girls	Boys / Girls	Bronze Boys / Girls
11	13.5 / 14.0	14.5 / 15.0	15.5 / 17.0
12	13.0 / 13.6	14.0 / 14.7	15.0 / 16.4
13	12.5 / 13.2	13.6 / 14.4	14.5 / 15.9
14	12.0 / 13.0	12.8 / 14.0	14.0 / 15.4
15	11.6 / 12.6	12.4 / 13.6	13.7 / 14.8
16+	11.4 / 12.4	12.0 / 13.2	13.4 / 14.4

200m

Age	Gold Boys / Girls	Silver Boys / Girls	Bronze Boys / Girls
11	28.0 / 29.5	30.5 / 33.5	34.0 / 37.0
12	27.6 / 28.5	29.5 / 32.5	32.0 / 35.5
13	25.5 / 27.0	28.5 / 31.5	31.0 / 34.0
14	24.5 / 26.5	27.0 / 29.0	30.0 / 33.0
15	23.5 / 25.8	26.0 / 28.0	29.0 / 32.0
16+	22.9 / 24.9	25.0 / 26.8	28.0 / 31.0

400m

Age	Gold Boys / Girls	Silver Boys / Girls	Bronze Boys / Girls
11	62.5 / 68.0	67.5 / 72.0	75.0 / 82.5
12	60.0 / 66.0	66.0 / 70.5	70.0 / 80.0
13	57.5 / 64.0	65.0 / 69.0	68.5 / 77.5
14	55.5 / 62.0	62.0 / 67.5	67.5 / 75.0
15	53.5 / 60.0	60.0 / 66.0	64.0 / 72.5
16+	52.5 / 58.0	57.0 / 65.0	62.0 / 70.0

Sprinting drills

The longer your stride length, the faster you can run. Stride length depends on good mobility, particularly in the hips. Exercises to improve this are shown on pages 36-37. Some drills to improve your speed and sprinting technique are shown here, and you could also use the knee lift and elbows drills on page 15.

Pick-ups

This technique is used to improve your acceleration and speed. It is best to do it on a track, as shown here.

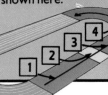

High knee lift

Rear leg extended

Front leg extended

Land on ball of foot

As your right leg swings forwards, your left leg should be fully extended behind. Lift your right knee up high, so that your thigh is parallel to the ground. This will enable you to achieve your maximum stride length.

As your right foot reaches forwards, pull it back slightly to strike the ground. Land on the ball of your foot. Your feet and knees should point straight ahead, and your neck and shoulders should be relaxed and steady.

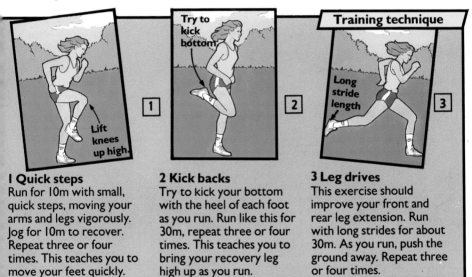

Training technique

Try to kick bottom

Lift knees up high.

Long stride length

1 **2** **3**

1 Quick steps
Run for 10m with small, quick steps, moving your arms and legs vigorously. Jog for 10m to recover. Repeat three or four times. This teaches you to move your feet quickly.

2 Kick backs
Try to kick your bottom with the heel of each foot as you run. Run like this for 30m, repeat three or four times. This teaches you to bring your recovery leg high up as you run.

3 Leg drives
This exercise should improve your front and rear leg extension. Run with long strides for about 30m. As you run, push the ground away. Repeat three or four times.

Speed training techniques

1 Start running slowly, then gradually accelerate. You should reach your top speed about half-way along the straight.

2 Run at top speed for 30m.

3 Gradually slow down to reach a jog at the end of the straight.

4 Walk round the bend, to repeat the pick-up on the other straight. Do 6-8 pick-ups in all.

Repetition running for speed

Some repetitions you could try are shown below. You should sprint the fast sections, and allow yourself a long recovery time so that you are fully recovered before attempting the next sprint.

★ 4 x 150m walk back to the start to recover.
★ 3 x 200m with 3 minute recoveries.

Sprinting: race tactics

Starting blocks are used in all sprint races to help you get off to a fast start. You will need to practise with the blocks before you use them in a race.

Below you can find out how to use the blocks and follow the starting commands. There are also tips on suitable tactics for the three sprint races.

Setting up your blocks

The blocks can be set in a number of different positions. You can alter the angle of the blocks and the distance between them, and you can move the blocks nearer to or further away from the starting line. An average setting would be to have the front block about two foot lengths behind the starting line, with the blocks one foot length apart and set to the angles shown on the right. However, it is worth experimenting with various settings to find one that suits you.

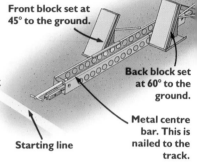

Front block set at 45° to the ground.

Back block set at 60° to the ground.

Metal centre bar. This is nailed to the track.

Starting line

Following the starting commands

In a sprint race there are three commands: "On your marks", "Set" and the starting pistol. The steps below will show you what to do on each command.

On your marks...

Look down at track

Hands behind line

Set...

Hips raised above shoulders

Go!

Push off hard with back foot

Swing arms

Back into the blocks and adopt a crouching position, Your toes should touch the track, with the balls of your feet on the blocks. Rest your hands on the ground behind the starting line, shoulder-width apart, with your fingers and thumb forming a bridge. Look down at the track.

On the command "Set", you should raise your hips up so that they are higher than your shoulders. Your arms should be straight and at right angles to the ground, with your shoulders above your hands. Concentrate on waiting for the sound of the starter's gun.

At the gun, remove your hands from the ground. Throw the arm opposite your rear leg forwards and your other arm backwards to help thrust you out of the blocks. Drive hard against the block with your front leg and bring your rear leg forwards to take the first stride.

False starts

If you leave the blocks before the gun has been fired, it counts as a false start and the race will be stopped. If you false start twice, you will be disqualified.

If you often false start, it may be because you are not properly balanced in your blocks. Adjust your position so that you are more stable.

The stages of a sprint race

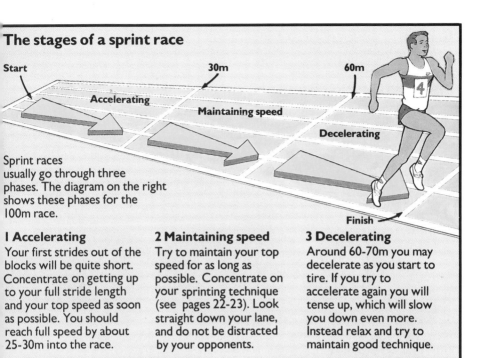

Start   30m   60m

Accelerating

Maintaining speed

Decelerating

Sprint races usually go through three phases. The diagram on the right shows these phases for the 100m race.

Finish

1 Accelerating
Your first strides out of the blocks will be quite short. Concentrate on getting up to your full stride length and your top speed as soon as possible. You should reach full speed by about 25-30m into the race.

2 Maintaining speed
Try to maintain your top speed for as long as possible. Concentrate on your sprinting technique (see pages 22-23). Look straight down your lane, and do not be distracted by your opponents.

3 Decelerating
Around 60-70m you may decelerate as you start to tire. If you try to accelerate again you will tense up, which will slow you down even more. Instead relax and try to maintain good technique.

The 200m and 400m races

In the 200m race, it is difficult to reach your top speed on the bend, so the acceleration phase will last into the straight. This means you will probably run the second 100m as fast as the first.

The 400m is the most tiring of all the sprints. To run this race well, you must spread your effort evenly. Practise until you can run the second half less than a second slower than the first half.

Running bends

In both the 200m and 400m races you have to run round bends. When you run at high speeds on a curve, you tend to be thrown towards the outside. This is worst in the inside lanes, where the curve is more pronounced. You must stay in your lane, close to the inside edge to run the shortest distance. The solution is to lean into the bend, as shown below.

Drop your left shoulder, swing your right arm across your body, and lean into the bend.

The finish

Sprinters often lean forwards at the end of a race. This is called a dip finish. It is used because, in a close finish, it is the runner whose torso crosses the line first who wins.

A correct dip finish is shown below. You must dip on the very last stride of the race – if you do it any earlier you will decelerate rapidly because you have stopped driving your arms.

On the last stride, thrust your chest forwards, and at the same time throw your arms back behind you.

Relays

A relay is a race in which four runners each run part of the total distance. The two most common relay races are the 4 x 100m and the 4 x 400m. Relays give you the opportunity to take part in a team event in what is otherwise an individual sport.

Passing the baton

A relay race depends on quick and efficient baton passing. If you drop the baton, or if the exchange slows you down, this will probably cost your team the race.

There are two ways to pass the baton, which are explained below*. The baton is always passed with both runners on the move to save time.

The visual pass (used in the 4 x 400m)

The receiver checks his route, then turns his head and upper body back to face the incoming runner.

He reaches back with his left arm and takes the baton from the incoming runner's right hand.

After a few strides, he will transfer the baton to his right hand, ready to pass to the next runner.

The blind pass (used in the 4 x 100m)

The incoming runner calls "Hand" when she is close enough to pass the baton to the receiver.

Without looking back, the receiver stretches his hand back and the incoming runner puts the baton into it.

To save time, runners do not transfer the baton to their other hand after receiving it.

The hand-over

The baton can be transferred from one runner's hand to the next in two ways: an upward or a downward sweep. These are shown below.

The upward sweep

The receiver stretches back his hand as shown. The incoming athlete places the baton upwards into the 'V' between the thumb and first finger.

The downward sweep

The receiver stretches back his hand with the palm upwards. The incoming athlete places the baton downwards into the palm.

*To distinguish between the two runners in the photos, the receiver is always male and the incoming runner is always female. Normally the members of a team are all the same sex.

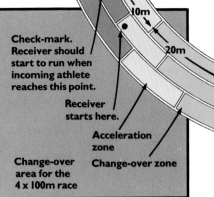

sing the change-over zone

e baton must be passed from one runner to the xt within a 20m change-over zone, which is marked the track. In the 4 × 100m race, receivers can also e a 10m acceleration zone, situated before the ange-over zone (see diagram). This helps them to ach maximum speed before the baton is passed.

The two runners must be going at the same speed, d be in the right positions to pass the baton in the ange-over zone. In training, experiment to find out hich point the incoming runner should reach when e receiver starts to run. You can mark this point on e track with tape before a race.

Check-mark. Receiver should start to run when incoming athlete reaches this point.

Receiver starts here.

Acceleration zone

Change-over area for the 4 x 100m race

Change-over zone

he order of runners

4 x 100m

The first runner must be a fast and reliable arter, to get the team into a good position.

The second runner must be good at baton ssing, as he has two exchanges to make. He often the fastest of the four.

The third runner should be good at bend nning and baton passing. A 200m specialist ideal.

The last runner must be determined to in and good at running under pressure, as e may have to make up any lost ground.

Change-overs in the 4 x 100m race

| 1st runner | ⇒ | 3rd runner | ⇒ |
| 2nd runner | ⇒ | 4th runner | ⇒ |

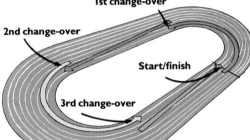

1st change-over

2nd change-over

Start/finish

3rd change-over

4 x 400m

The first runner should e a good starter and used o running in lanes.

The second athlete ns the first bend in lane, d can then break for the side. He should be repared to fight for a ood position in the inside ne.

The third runner waits a jostling line of runners. e must try to hold off the ther waiting runners with s arm to make space for s incoming team-mate.

The fourth runner ould be the fastest in the am.

Relay targets

4 x 100m (times in seconds)			
Age	Gold Boys / Girls	Silver Boys / Girls	Bronze Boys / Girls
11	53.5 / 55.5	57.5 / 59.5	61.0 / 67.0
12	51.5 / 54.0	55.5 / 58.0	59.5 / 65.0
13	49.5 / 52.0	53.5 / 56.5	57.5 / 63.0
14	47.5 / 51.0	51.0 / 55.5	55.5 / 61.0
15	46.0 / 50.0	49.5 / 54.0	54.0 / 59.0
16+	45.0 / 49.5	47.5 / 52.5	53.0 / 58.0

4 x 400m (times in minutes)			
Age	Gold Boys / Girls	Silver Boys / Girls	Bronze Boys / Girls
11	4:03 / 4:28	4:26 / 4:44	4:56 / 5:25
12	3:56 / 4:20	4:20 / 4:38	4:36 / 5:16
13	3:46 / 4:12	4:16 / 4:32	4:30 / 5:06
14	3:38 / 4:04	4:04 / 4:26	4:26 / 4:56
15	3:34 / 3:56	3:56 / 4:20	4:12 / 4:46
16+	3:26 / 3:48	3:44 / 4:16	4:04 / 4:36

Hurdling

A hurdles race is a sprint race which also involves getting over up to ten obstacles. To be a successful hurdler, you must first be a good sprinter and then master the additional technique of clearing the hurdles.

There are two hurdle events – the 110m (100m for women) and the 400m. In junior meetings shorter distances, such as 60m or 80m, are also run. The number, height and distance between the hurdles varies according to the race. For example, the hurdles in the 400m are generally lower than those in the 110m because the longer race is more tiring.

About hurdles

A hurdle consists of a metal frame supporting a wooden cross bar. When you first start hurdling, this may seem a rather daunting obstacle. In fact it is quite safe, as it is designed to fall over if you knock it. If you watch a hurdles race, you will see that athletes often knock down several hurdles and continue running without injury. Hurdles are only dangerous if you approach them from the wrong side, as shown in the diagrams on the right.

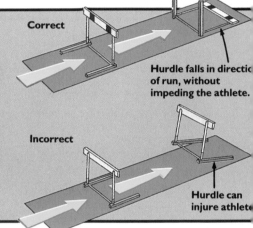

Correct

Hurdle falls in direction of run, without impeding the athlete.

Incorrect

Hurdle can injure athlete

Hurdling technique

You are slower in the air than when running, so the faster you can clear each hurdle the better your finishing time will be. Concentrate on keeping as low as possible over the hurdles and on running rather than jumping over them.

Knee bent

Trail leg pulled up

Land on lead leg

Trail leg brought round

Pick up your lead leg* with the knee bent and reach forward with your opposite arm**. As you pass over the hurdle, straighten your lead leg and bring your trail leg round to the side, with your heel held by your bottom and your knee pulled up and out.

Try to bring your lead leg down to the ground as quickly as possible so that you can run off the hurdle. As your trail foot passes over the hurdle, pull your knee and foot round to the sprinting position. This enables you to run off the hurdle and continue your normal sprinting action.

*Your lead leg is the one that goes over the hurdle first.
**Female hurdlers often adopt a more upright position than men at this point.*

Hurdling targets (times in seconds)

Age	Distance	Gold Boys / Girls	Silver Boys / Girls	Bronze Boys / Girls
11	80m / 75m	14.0 / 13.5	14.8 / 14.5	16.4 / 16.5
12	80m / 75m	13.4 / 13.0	14.0 / 14.0	15.5 / 16.0
13	80m / 75m	12.8 / 12.5	13.5 / 13.5	15.0 / 15.5
14	80m / 75m	12.4 / 12.0	13.0 / 13.0	14.5 / 15.0
15	100m / 80m	15.0 / 12.7	16.0 / 13.5	17.5 / 15.5
16+	100m / 80m	14.5 / 12.5	15.5 / 13.3	17.0 / 15.0

Stride patterns

Sprinting between the hurdles is not haphazard – you have to use a set stride pattern in order to take off at the same distance from each hurdle. You should work out your stride pattern in training.

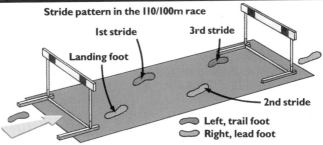

Stride pattern in the 110/100m race

1st stride   3rd stride

Landing foot

2nd stride

Left, trail foot
Right, lead foot

In the 110/100m race, hurdlers use three strides between hurdles. This lets you tackle each hurdle with the same lead leg (see diagram above).

Hurdlers in the 400m race have to use a more flexible stride pattern. As the race progresses, they start to tire, their stride length shortens and they may have to take an extra stride to reach the later hurdles. This is often referred to as changing down.

Most male 400m hurdlers take about 14 or 15 strides between hurdles, changing down to 15 or 16 strides later in the race. You should practise changing down in training, so that you know where to do it. You will need to be able to lead with both legs to do this during a race.

Hurdling drills

Try the drills below to improve your hurdling technique. You will need good hip mobility (see pages 36-37) to be able to perform the hurdling action.

Training technique

1 Before tackling full-size hurdles, practise on something smaller. You could start with lines on the ground, then move on to a low obstacle, such as the one shown here. Concentrate on running over the hurdle.

Support – this could be bricks or a waste-paper bin.

Raise the supports as you improve.

Bamboo cane

2 Work on your lead leg action by running at the side of the hurdles and clearing each one with just your lead leg. Concentrate on throwing your leg at the hurdle and taking the same number of steps between the hurdles.

3 Work on your trail leg action by running at the other side of the hurdles and clearing the hurdle with just your trail leg. Concentrate on pulling your knee up, and then bringing your knee and foot round to the front.

Steeplechase

A steeplechase was originally a race for horses in which a series of barriers had to be jumped. In 1850 Halifax Wyatt, a student at Oxford University, bet some friends that he could complete a steeplechase course better on foot than on a horse, and so the first race took place. Nowadays, the steeplechase is a 3,000m race which takes place on the track. At present this event is contested only by men.

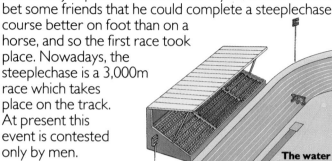

The water jump may be on the inside or outside of the track.

The course

During a steeplechase race, runners have to negotiate two types of obstacles: solid wooden barriers and a water jump. On each circuit of the track there are four barriers and one water jump, usually arranged as shown on the right. The water jump consists of a wooden barrier, in front of a 3.66m square trough of water. The trough has a maximum depth of 70cm at the barrier, but slopes up to the track.

Water jump

Wooden barrier

Getting over the obstacles

You are allowed to get over the obstacles in two ways: you can either hurdle, or step on them. These two methods are explained here.

The technique shown here is incorrect.

The athlete's trail leg will not pass over the barrier.

Hurdling

This is the most efficient way to clear the barriers, as you do not lose speed or break your running rhythm. The technique is broadly the same as in sprint hurdling (see page 28). However, you should not skim over the top of the barrier – if you knock it you could injure yourself badly. It is safer to go higher than with a normal hurdle.

You should practise leading with both legs to make you more versatile. Be careful not to trail a leg round the outside of the barriers (see diagram on the left), as you could be disqualified for this.

Stepping on the obstacles

You should always use this technique for the water jump, and you can also use it for the barriers (see photos) if you are too tired to hurdle. To avoid injury or getting wet, you could practise your technique with a barrier placed in front of the long jump pit. This will give you a soft landing area.

Lean forwards and drive up and forwards on to the barrier. Place your lead foot firmly on top of the barrier, and use your arms to help you keep your balance as you swing your trail leg up and through.

Stay in a crouched position to keep your centre of gravity low as you pass over the barrier. As you push off, try to keep your foot in contact with the barrier for as long as possible to push yourself forwards.

Race tactics

★ Aim to run the race at a steady pace. Avoid accelerating or decelerating at the barriers, as this saps your energy.

★ At the start of the race there is a clear run before the officials place the barriers on the track. This is to let the runners spread out. Try to get to the front, and to get into a space so that you will have a clear run at the obstacles.

★ If you do get caught behind other runners at a barrier, either move out into one of the outer lanes, or slow down to let them get over before you.

★ Hurdle the barriers when possible, but if you start to tire, step on them.

★ Don't try to leap right over the water. This uses a lot of energy and is likely to disrupt your rhythm. Land with your leading foot on the slope, so that your trail foot lands on the dry track to continue running.

Training techniques

Interval training

You can adapt interval training for steeplechase by including some barriers in your run. This will help to build up your endurance. You could try the session shown below.

Run on the track.

Hurdle the barriers.

Jog across the grass to recover.

Do 6-10 sessions of 200m with a recovery jog, as shown above.

Steeplechase targets (times in minutes)

Age	Distance	Gold	Silver	Bronze
13*	1000m	3:20	3:40	4:10
14	1000m	3:10	3:30	4:00
15	1500m	4:48	5:18	5:54
16+	1500m	4:40	5:03	5:48

*Runners under 13 should not attempt the steeplechase, as it is very strenuous.

Running shoes

The purpose of running shoes is to cushion your feet and legs from the jarring action of running. Other sports shoes do not provide this protection, and can result in injury.

On these two pages you can read about the different types of shoe available, and about some of the features you should look for when choosing them.

Tips on buying running shoes

★ Always go to a sports shop where the assistants know about running and can advise you on suitable shoes.

★ Explain which sort of running you are taking part in, and roughly how far you expect to run each week. An athlete who runs 100km per week will need more hard-wearing shoes than a jogger who runs only 5km per week.

★ Lace the shoes up and walk around in them in the shop to test that they are comfortable.

★ It is best to buy shoes during the afternoon. Your feet tend to swell up during the day and will be bigger in the afternoon than in the morning.

★ Wear your sports socks when trying on shoes.

★ Always buy shoes that feel comfortable when you try them on. Don't rely on them stretching or softening up with wear.

★ Always break your shoes in on short training runs – don't use them for the first time in a race.

What the jargon means

Dual density mid-sole An area of denser material has been inserted in the mid-sole to prevent your foot from rolling too far sideways on landing. 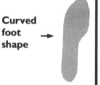 **Wedge**	**Slip-lasted** This describes a shoe which is made with no board in it. This makes the shoe much lighter and more flexible. **Upper**
Curve-lasted A curve-lasted shoe is made on a last (a model of a foot) which curves inwards from the heel to the toes. **Curved foot shape** →	**Variable width lacing** The lace holes are staggered, rather than in a line. This lets you adjust the fit of the upper to the width of your foot. **Wide feet** **Narrow feet**
Straight-lasted Some people have feet which do not curve inwards. Special shoes are made on a straight last for this shape of foot. **Straight foot shape** →	**Achilles' heel dip** This is a heel tab which has been cut down to avoid putting pressure on the back of your heel (the Achilles tendon). **Heel dip**
Board-lasted The upper is usually stretched over a last and glued to a flexible board. A board-lasted shoe gives your foot a lot of support. **Upper** **Board** 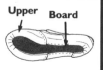	**Waffle sole** This is a pattern of square studs on the outer sole of training shoes. It gives good grip on soft or uneven ground. **Waffles**

Trainers

Trainers are the most common running shoes, as they are used for both jogging and road racing. Track runners may also wear them when they are training. The diagram below shows the main parts of a trainer and explains their functions.

Heel tab to protect the back of your ankle and Achilles tendon.

Heel counter – a semi-circular support wrapped around the back of the shoe. It holds your heel in a steady position.

Mesh or nylon upper to let sweat escape.

Outer-sole made of hard-wearing rubber to provide grip.

Mid-sole – this provides cushioning for your foot.

What to look for in a training shoe

★ Make sure the shoes are big enough, as your feet expand a lot during exercise. Press at the end of your big toe – there should be a thumb's width between your toe and the end of the shoe.

★ It should have a completely rigid heel counter to hold your foot in place. Test by squeezing it between your thumb and forefinger – it should not give way.

★ A stiff heel tab can damage your Achilles tendon. Hold the shoe by its heel tab – it should flop forwards if the tab is soft enough.

★ Test the mid-sole to make sure it will cushion you by pressing it with your finger. It should feel squidgy.

★ Look for good grip on the outer-sole, such as a waffle or ripple pattern.

Other types of running shoe

If you take part in track or cross-country races, you will need a pair of specialized shoes in addition to your trainers. The tips below will show you what to look for.

Spike shoes

Sprinter's shoe →

Middle distance shoe →

Cross-country shoes

Spike shoe suitable for cross-country running.

These are used on track surfaces and grass. The sole has fittings for a number of spikes, which provide grip. These come in a variety of lengths: the harder the surface, the shorter the spike you need*. There are two types of spike shoe: distance spikes, which have a wedge-shaped heel, and sprinting spikes, which have no heel. Spike shoes should be very light and should fit closely. Avoid shoes with built-in spikes. Instead choose a pair with a spike plate, so that you can use spikes of different lengths.

The best shoes to wear for cross-country running will depend on the nature of the course. If the ground is likely to be quite hard or if there are roads in the course, wear a pair of trainers with good sole grips. If the course is likely to be very muddy, spikes will give you the best grip. Use a pair of middle distance spikes with well-cushioned heels, and choose a spike length of 12-15mm (but check first that there are not going to be any long stretches of road on the course).

*Recommended lengths are: up to 6mm on synthetic tracks, up to 13mm on cinder tracks and up to 15mm on grass.

Foot problems

Few people have a perfect running style. In fact many successful runners have a slightly awkward gait, which often results in them landing incorrectly on their feet. Eventually, this can lead to injuries. For example, if your foot rolls too far in one direction, this puts your leg in an awkward position and often results in damage to your leg or knee.

Below you can read about two of these problems, and about what you can do to correct them.

Pronation and supination

The most common problem is when your foot rolls too far towards the inside as it pushes off. This is called pronation. If you tend to pronate, your shoes will eventually cave in on the inside.

The opposite problem, of your foot rolling towards the outside, is called supination. If you tend to supinate, your shoes will cave in on the outside. This is much less common than pronation.

If you suspect that you might pronate or supinate, it is a good idea to take your old shoes along to the shop when you buy a new pair. The assistant will be able to check how they have worn and advise you on a suitable replacement pair to help ease the problem. For example, many shoes now have a special wedge of denser material built into the mid-sole to encourage you to land in the right position.

Experienced runners who suffer from these problems often use special inner soles,

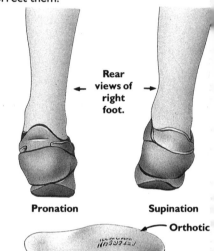

Rear views of right foot.

Pronation   Supination

Orthotic

called orthotics, to correct their tendency to pronate or supinate. An orthotic is a piece of foam or plastic which fits inside your shoe and forces your foot to strike the ground at the correct angle.

Looking after your shoes

★ If your shoes get wet and muddy, wash the outside with warm, soapy water, rinse off all the suds, stuff the shoes with newspaper to help them keep their shape, and leave them to dry naturally.

★ Some shoes can be cleaned in a washing machine set to a low temperature, but you should check the manufacturer's instructions before you try this.

★ Check your shoes regularly for signs of wear. Check that the mid-sole still feels squidgy when squeezed – eventually it will become compressed and will no longer cushion your foot. When this happens you should buy a new pair of shoes.

★ You should also check that you have not worn through the outer-sole of the shoe. It is possible to have this replaced by a specialist shoe repair company, which is much cheaper than buying a new pair of shoes. Your local sports shop or a specialist running magazine may be able to put you in touch with a company that provides this service.

★ If your spike shoes get wet, remove the spikes while you leave them to dry. When you replace the spikes, spread some vaseline on the threads to stop the spikes rusting into the spike plate. Replace any worn or broken spikes with new ones.

Running kit

It is not necessary to spend a lot of money on special clothes for running – apart from your shoes, all you need to get started are a T-shirt, some shorts and a pair of sports socks. However, there are many clothes made especially for runners which can be useful, particularly if you run in cold weather. You can read about these below.

Shorts

Look for a pair of light-weight nylon or cotton and polyester shorts, which are hard-wearing and easy to wash. Some come with built-in briefs. Try the shorts on in the shop, and try out a range of movements to make sure they are not tight or restrictive.

Tops

A loose-fitting T-shirt is ideal for running, and can also be worn under a track suit in colder weather. In hot weather you may prefer to wear a light-weight singlet (a runner's vest). Look for one made from a mix of cotton and polyester or from nylon. Pure cotton singlets are not so good, as they absorb sweat and get very heavy. A mesh panel in the singlet will help sweat to evaporate. Try the singlet on in the shop and move your arms around to make sure it does not restrict movement.

Thermals

Thermal clothes are made from synthetic fibres which trap your body heat, but allow sweat to evaporate. A long-sleeved thermal top and a pair of thermal running tights are ideal for training in cold weather. You can wear them under shorts and a singlet, or under a tracksuit. If possible, try them on in the shop to make sure that they do not irritate your skin and are not too tight under the arms.

Stop-watch

A digital wrist-watch with a stop-watch built in is useful for timing your runs. Specialist runners' watches can also count laps and store your lap times.

Socks

When choosing socks, look for an absorbent material, such as cotton or wool, with some man-made fibre added to make it more hard-wearing. Check that there are no seams across the heel or toes which could rub your foot and cause blisters.

Track suits

Track suits are ideal for keeping you warm before and after running. They are also useful for training in cold weather, but make sure that the top won't ride up from the trousers.

Tracksters

These are nylon running trousers which you can put on and take off easily over running shoes. They are very hard-wearing and easy to wash, and can be used for winter training sessions.

Rain suits

These suits are designed to keep you warm and dry in wet or windy weather. The cheaper suits are made of waterproof nylon which keeps rain out, but also traps sweat inside, so you can get very hot and sticky. Other rain suits are made from materials such as *Gortex*, which breathe – they resist rain but let sweat out. However, suits made of these materials can be extremely expensive.

Extras

A sweat-band is useful in hot weather to stop sweat running into your eyes. In cold weather you will need a hat and gloves to keep your head and hands warm.

Warm-up and mobility exercises

It is important to warm up before running, as this prepares your body for exercise. It also helps you avoid injuries, as warm muscles are less likely to tear or strain than cold ones. Mobility exercises gently stretch your muscles and tendons, making a wider range of joint movements possible.

Mobility exercises

These exercises are stretches designed to increase the range of movement in the joints you use for running. You should hold each stretch for about five seconds and then relax before repeating it. You could include some mobility exercises in your warm-up routine.

Warming up

Start your warm-up by jogging for about 800m. Then move on to some gentle exercises like the ones shown here*, to stretch your muscles. You should hold each stretch for about five seconds and then relax before repeating it. Finish with about six pick-ups (see page 23) over a distance of 50-80m, to get your body used to running fast.

Calf muscles

Stand in front of a wall and take one stride backwards. Lean forwards and place your hands against the wall. Keeping your body straight, press your heels to the floor, stretching your calf muscles. Repeat five times.

Push your heels down.

Hamstrings

Stand on your left leg and support your right leg on a chair. Keeping both legs straight, stretch forward and hold your right foot, or as far down your leg as you can reach. Hold for five seconds and repeat five times on each leg.

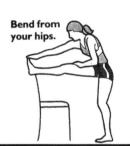

Bend from your hips.

Ankles

Sit with your legs stretched out in front of you. Push your toes as far away from your body as possible, then pull them towards you. Repeat ten times.

Push your toes towards the floor.

Hips

Lie on your back. Lift one leg up, grasp it behind the knee and pull it towards your chest. Try to straighten your leg. Repeat five times with each leg.

Pull your leg to your chest.

Hips

Sit with your leg stretched out on a bench. Bend forwards, and try to lower your upper body on to your leg. Repeat five times with each leg.

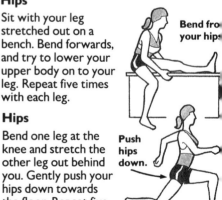

Bend from your hips

Hips

Bend one leg at the knee and stretch the other leg out behind you. Gently push your hips down towards the floor. Repeat five times with each leg.

Push hips down.

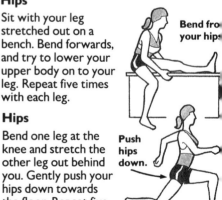

You could also include the exercises shown on page 10.

Trunk muscles

Raise your left arm above your head and bend to the right. Avoid leaning forwards or backwards. Hold for five seconds, then straighten up. Repeat five times on each side.

Stretch to the side.

Lower back muscles

Lie face-down on the floor, with your hands under your shoulders.

Push your body upwards.

Keeping your hips on the ground, look up at the ceiling and push up to raise your upper body. Repeat five times.

Shoulder muscles

Holding your arms straight, swing them gently in large circular movements. Swing your arms forwards for about ten seconds, then swing them backwards.

Rotate arms.

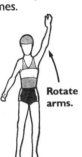

Ankles

Sit with your right leg stretched out in front of you. Hold your left leg in your arms so that the lower leg hangs loosely, then rotate your left foot ten times in each direction. Repeat with the other foot.

Rotate this foot.

Inside of thighs

Sit on the floor and place the soles of your feet together. Pull your feet up towards your body. Then gently press your knees down towards the floor. Repeat five times.

Press knees downwards.

Warming down

Always remember to warm down at the end of your run. Start your warm-down with some easy stretching exercises like the ones shown above. Move on to some gentle jogging to help flush any lactic acid out of your muscles (see page 7).

Mobility exercises for hurdlers

Bend forwards from your hips.

Keep your leg straight.

Swing this leg.

Sit on the floor in the hurdling position. Reach forwards, and move your hands in a semi-circle from your trail leg to your lead leg. Repeat five times with each leg.

Place the lower part of your left leg along a hurdle. Keeping your right leg straight, bend forwards and reach for your right ankle. Repeat five times with each leg.

Hold on to a hurdle to help you keep your balance. Stand on your right leg and swing your left foot from side to side in front of you ten times. Repeat with your other leg.

Strength training

The stronger your muscles are, the better you will be able to cope with regular running and training. Powerful muscles help you to run faster, and to keep going for longer. They are also less likely to strain or rip than weak, untrained muscles.

All top runners therefore include some strength work as part of their training routine. Two simple strength routines you can try yourself are plyometrics and circuit training, both of which are illustrated below.

Plyometrics

Plyometrics is a general term used to describe hopping, jumping or bounding exercises. These are strength exercises which work specifically on the leg muscles. They are particularly good for sprinters, as they also increase the speed at which your leg muscles contract, which helps you to run faster.

To try plyometrics, you could hop, jump, skip or bound for 20m, building up to 30m as you improve. You should do two or three repetitions of each exercise.

Bounding   **Jumping**   **Hopp**

Your pulse rate

When you exercise, your heart beats faster in order to pump more blood to your muscles. The rate at which your heart beats (called your pulse) is a good guide to the intensity of the work you are doing. Taking your pulse during a training session will show you how hard you are working.

How to take your pulse

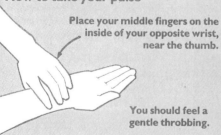

Place your middle fingers on the inside of your opposite wrist, near the thumb.

You should feel a gentle throbbing.

Using a watch or clock with a second hand, count how many beats you feel in 15 seconds. Then multiply this by four to find your pulse rate per minute.

Your pulse rate and training

In order to achieve any benefit from aerobic training, you have to exercise hard enough to raise your pulse to a certain level, called the training threshold. The steps below will show you how to find your training threshold.

1 Take your resting pulse rate before you warm up.

2 After you warm up, run as fast as you can for 300m. Then take your pulse again.

3 The difference between the two rates is your pulse range.

4 Your training threshold is your resting pulse rate plus two-thirds of your pulse range.

If you train regularly, you will find that you can do the same amount of exercise with less effort. You will need to do more in order to keep your pulse around the training threshold and to continue improving your fitness.

Circuit training

Circuit training is used to develop your general strength and stamina. It consists of a course which you either walk or run around, stopping at various points to do a series of exercises. A typical circuit you could try is shown below. You could do it in a park or field, or indoors in a hall or gym.

Press-ups

Lie face down with your hands beneath your shoulders. Keeping your back straight, push with your hands to raise your body. Lower your body almost to the ground, then repeat.*

Keep your body straight.

Sit-ups

Lie on your back with your knees bent and your hands held on your shoulders. Slowly lift your upper body until your elbows touch your knees. Then lower your body again. It may help if someone holds your feet.

Lift your upper body.

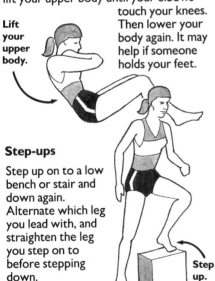

Step-ups

Step up on to a low bench or stair and down again. Alternate which leg you lead with, and straighten the leg you step on to before stepping down.

Step up.

Squat thrusts

Crouch on all fours with your hands on the ground, shoulder-width apart. Without moving your hands, jump your feet backwards to extend your legs and forwards to bring your knees up to your elbows.

Jump feet backwards.

Back raise

Lie on your front, with your hands clasped behind your head. Slowly arch your back to raise your head and upper body from the floor. Then lower your body again. It may help if someone holds your legs down.

Arch your back.

Dips

Position yourself as shown in the diagram, supporting yourself on a chair or bench. Keeping your body straight, bend and straighten your arms to lower and raise your body.

Raise and lower body.

Do each of the exercises for 30 seconds, followed by a 30 second recovery period. Use the recovery time to walk to the next exercise. As you get fitter, you could run between exercises to make the circuit more difficult.

When you have completed the circuit, rest for five minutes before continuing. Start with three complete circuits and build up to six as you get fitter.

If you find this very difficult, try press-ups from a kneeling position.

Annual training programmes

To do well in competitions, you need to reach your peak fitness and performance at the right time. In order to achieve this, your training must be carefully planned throughout the year.

The training year

The training year divides into four phases, shown here:

1 General training. To build up your general level of fitness, your training should include running lots of different distances, not just the ones you intend to race, as well as mobility exercises, plyometrics and circuit training to increase your fitness and stamina.

2 Training for competition. Continue to work on your general fitness, but also start to train specifically for your event.

Concentrate on technique, building up your speed, improving your start and interval training suited to your event.

3 Competition period. Reduce your training to keep you fresh for the competitions. Your training should aim merely to maintain the level of fitness and performance which you achieved in the previous phase.

4 Recovery period. This is an annual break from training. If you want to keep up your fitness, try other sports.

Dividing up your year

The diagrams below show how long each phase should last, according to which competitions you are training for. As competition periods are linked to the seasons (cross-country usually takes place in winter and track and field in summer, for example), they fall in different months in different parts of the world. On the diagrams, 'month 1' means the first month of the training year. You can see which calendar month this is in the key.

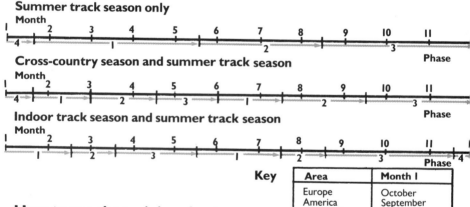

Summer track season only

Cross-country season and summer track season

Indoor track season and summer track season

Key	Area	Month 1
	Europe	October
	America	September
	Australasia	May

How to use the training charts

The charts opposite are designed to help you plan a whole year's training. They describe a typical week's training in each phase. You will not want to repeat this same training every week for several months. Instead use the chart to get an idea of the type and amount of running you should be doing in each phase.

The training techniques and exercises suggested are explained earlier in this book, and page references are given in the charts. Anything marked with an asterisk is explained in the key at the end of the charts.

Age 11-12 (two sessions per week maximum)

Sprinters	Endurance runners	Hurdlers

Phase 1 – General training

Session 1
- ★ Running drills (page 15)
- ★ 6 x run 100m then walk 100m

Session 2
- ★ Mobility exercises (pages 36-37) and circuit training (page 39)
- ★ 12 mins running

Endurance runners:
- ★ Running drills (page 15)
- ★ 8 x run 100m then jog 100m
- ★ Mobility exercises (pages 36-37) and circuit training (page 39)
- ★ 15 mins running

Hurdlers:
- ★ Running drills (page 15)
- ★ 6 x run 100m then walk 100m
- ★ Mobility exercises (pages 36-37) and circuit training (page 39)
- ★ 12 mins running

Phase 2 – Training for competition

Session 1
- ★ Sprint drills (page 23)
- ★ 4 x 30m block starts*
- ★ 4 x 60m sprints
- ★ Plyometrics (page 38)

Session 2
- ★ Mobility exercises (pages 36-37) and circuit training (page 39)
- ★ 6 x 50m hill running (page 11)

Endurance runners:
- ★ Running drills (page 15)
- ★ 4 x 200m run with 200m jog recovery
- ★ Plyometrics (page 38)
- ★ Mobility exercises (pages 36-37) and circuit training (page 39)
- ★ 15-20 mins running

Hurdlers:
- ★ Hurdle drills (page 29)
- ★ 4 x block start* plus 3h*
- ★ 2 x 5h timed*
- ★ Plyometrics (page 38)
- ★ Mobility exercises (page 36-37) and circuit training (page 39)
- ★ 6 x 50m hill running (page 11)

Phase 3 – Competition

Session 1
- ★ Sprint drills (page 23)
- ★ 5 x 30m block starts*
- ★ 2 x 60m timed sprint*

Session 2
- ★ Competition

Endurance runners:
- ★ Sprint drills (page 23)
- ★ 3 x 50m sprints
- ★ 4 x 150m with 2 min recovery
- ★ Competition

Hurdlers:
- ★ Hurdle drills (page 29)
- ★ 5 x block starts* plus 3h*
- ★ 2 x 6h timed sprint*
- ★ Competition

Age 13-14 (three sessions per week maximum)

Sprinters	Endurance runners	Hurdlers

Phase 1 – General training

Session 1
- ★ Running drills (page 15)
- ★ 6 x 150m run and 50m walk

Session 2
- ★ Mobility exercises (pages 36-37) and circuit training (page 39)
- ★ 15 mins running

Session 3
- ★ 6 x 50m sprints
- ★ 2 sets of 4 x 80m hill running (page 11)

Endurance runners:
- ★ Running drills (page 15)
- ★ 8 x 150m run and 150m jog
- ★ Mobility exercises (pages 36-37) and circuit training (page 39)
- ★ 20 mins running
- ★ 6 x 50m sprints
- ★ 3 x 4 min runs

Hurdlers:
- ★ Running drills (page 15)
- ★ 6 x 150m run and 50m walk
- ★ Mobility exercises (pages 36-37) and circuit training (page 39)
- ★ 15 mins running
- ★ Hurdle drills (page 29)
- ★ 2 sets of 4 x 80m hill running (page 11)

Phase 2 – training for competition

Session 1
- ★ Running drills (page 15)
- ★ 2 sets of 3 x 120m, walk back to recover, 12 mins rest between sets

Endurance runners:
- ★ Running drills (page 15)
- ★ 4 x 400m with 2 mins recovery

Hurdlers:
- ★ Running drills (page 15)
- ★ 2 sets of 3 x 120m, walk back to recover, 12 mins rest between sets

(continued on next page)

Session 2
★ Mobility exercises (pages 36-37), circuit training and plyometrics (pages 38-39)
★ 15 mins run
Session 3
★ Sprint drills (page 23)
★ 5 x 50m sprints
★ 2 sets of 4 x 50m hill running (page 11)

★ Mobility exercises (pages 36-37), circuit training and plyometrics (pages 38-39)
★ 20-30 mins run

★ 20 mins fartlek (page 11), or cross-country run (pages 12-13), or road race (page 9)

★ Mobility exercises (pages 36-37), circuit training and plyometrics (pages 38-39)
★ 15 mins run

★ Hurdle drills (page 29)
★ 5 x 100m with 5h*
★ 2 sets of 4 x 50m hill running (page 11)

Phase 3 – Competition period

Session 1
★ Sprint drills (page 23)
★ 6 x 30m block starts*
★ 2 sets of 120m, 90m then 60m

Session 2
★ 4 x 30m block starts*
★ 2 x 60m timed sprints*

Session 3
★ Competition

★ Sprint drills (page 23)
★ 5 x 200m with 4 mins recovery
★ 4 x 50m sprints

★ 4 x 120m sprint, walk back to recover
★ 15 mins run

★ Competition

★ Hurdle drills (page 29)
★ 6 x block start and 3h*
★ 4 x timed run over 5h*

★ 4 x block start and 3h*
★ 4 x last 4h* and sprint to finish line

★ Competition

Age 15-16+ (four sessions per week maximum)

Sprinters

Endurance runners

Hurdlers

Phase 1 – General training

Session 1
★ Running drills (page 15)
★ 6 laps of 400m track, jogging the straights and running the bends
Session 2
★ Mobility exercises (pages 36-37) and circuit training (page 39)
★ 15-20 mins run
Session 3
★ Sprint drills (page 23)
★ 2 sets of 5 x 80m hill running (page 11)
Session 4
★ 6 x 50m sprints
★ 2 sets of 4 x 150m, walk back to recover, 10 mins rest between sets

★ Running drills (page 15)
★ 4 x 1,000m with 3 mins recovery

★ Mobility exercises (pages 36-37) and circuit training (page 39)
★ 20-30 mins run

★ Running drills (page 15)
★ 2 sets of 6 x 80m hill running (page 11)

★ 20-30 mins fartlek (page 11) or cross-country race (page 12-13)

★ Running drills (page 15)
★ 6 laps of 400m track, jogging the straights and running the bends

★ Mobility exercises (pages 36-37) and circuit training (page 39)
★ 15-20 mins run

★ Hurdle drills (page 29)
★ 2 sets of 5 x 80m hill running (page 11)

★ 6 x 50m sprints
★ 2 sets of 4 x 150m, walk back to recover, 10 mins rest between sets

Phase 2 – Training for competition

Session 1
★ Running drills (page 15)
★ 2 sets of 250m, 200m then 150m, 2-3 mins recovery and 12 mins rest between sets
Session 2
★ Mobility exercises (pages 36-37) and circuit training (page 39)
★ 15-20 mins run

★ Running drills (page 15)
★ 2 sets of 4 x 300m, 2 mins recovery and 12 mins rest between sets

★ Mobility exercises (pages 36-37) and circuit training (page 39)
★ 20-30 mins run

★ Running drills (page 15)
★ 2 sets of 250m, 200m then 150m, 2-3 mins recovery and 12 mins rest between sets

★ Mobility exercises (pages 36-37) and circuit training (page 39)
★ 15-20 mins run

(continued on next page)

Session 3
* ★ Sprint drills (page 23)
* ★ 2 sets of 4 x 90m
* ★ Plyometrics (page 38)

Session 4
* ★ 8 x block starts*
* ★ 2 sets of 5 x 50m hill running
(page 11)

* ★ 6 x 50m sprints
* ★ 4 x 600m with 5 mins
recovery

* ★ 20-30 mins fartlek (page 11),
or cross country run (pages
12-13), or road race (page 9)

* ★ Hurdle drills (page 29)
* ★ 2 sets of 4 runs over 5h*
* ★ Plyometrics (page 38)

* ★ 8 x block starts*
* ★ 2 sets of 5 x 50m hill running
(page 11)

Phase 3 – Competition period

Session 1
* ★ Sprint drills (page 23)
* ★ 5 x 30m block starts*
* ★ 3 x 60m timed sprints*

* ★ Sprint drills (page 23)
* ★ 2 x 600m with 20 mins
recovery

* ★ Hurdle drills (page 29)
* ★ 5 x block start and 3h*
* ★ 3 timed runs over 5h*

Session 2
* ★ 6 x 30m block starts*
* ★ 200m, 150m then 80m at full
effort

* ★ 20-30 mins run
* ★ Plyometrics (page 38)

* ★ Starts – 2 x 2h*, 3h, 4h
* ★ 4 x last 4h and sprint to finish
line

Session 3
* ★ Sprint drills (page 23)
* ★ 2 sets of 3 x 90m acc runs*

* ★ Running drills (page 15)
* ★ 2 sets of 4 x 150m, 2 mins
recovery, 15 mins rest between
sets

* ★ Hurdle drills
* ★ 2 x 8h timed run*

Session 4
* ★ Competition

* ★ Competition

* ★ Competition

Key

Acc run = a run in which you
accelerate from jogging up to full
speed.

3h run = a run during which you
clear three hurdles.
Block start = start from the
blocks (see page 24) and sprint
the specified distance.

Timed sprint = sprint the
specified distance and get
someone else to time you.
Compare your times each week
to see how you are improving.

Conversion chart

All the measurements in this book are in
metric. If you prefer to use the imperial
system, you can either do a rough
conversion by substituting yards for
metres each time a measurement is given,
or you can use the chart below.

This conversion chart does not cover
every possible distance, only the ones
mentioned in the book. All the imperial
conversions have been rounded to the
nearest yard to make the distances
simpler to work out.

Metric	Imperial	Metric	Imperial	Metric	Imperial
6mm	0.24in	100m	109yd	2,400m	1ml 864yd
13mm	0.51in	110m	120yd	2,800m	1ml 1,301yd
15mm	0.59in	150m	164yd	3,000m	1ml 1,520yd
		200m	219yd	3,200m	1ml 1,738yd
30cm	1ft	300m	328yd	3,600m	2ml 416yd
70cm	2ft 4in	400m	437yd	4,000m	2ml 854yd
		800m	875yd	4,400m	2ml 1,291yd
10m	11yd	1,000m	1,094yd	4,800m	2ml 1,728yd
20m	22yd	1,200m	1,312yd	5,000m	3ml 188yd
30m	33yd	1,500m	1,640yd	6,500m	4ml 68yd
50m	55yd	1,600m	1,749yd	1,000m	6ml 376yd
60m	66yd	2,000m	1ml 427yd	100km	62ml 241yd
70m	77yd				
75m	82yd				
80m	87yd				

Abbreviations used: mm = millimetre, cm = centimetre,
m = metre, km = kilometre; in = inch, ft = foot, yd = yard,
ml = mile.

Taking part in a competition

If you are about to enter your first race, you may be wondering what to take with you and what to expect when you arrive at the competition. The tips below will prepare you for your racing début.

The day before

★ Pack your kit bag, so that you don't forget anything in a last minute rush. Use the list on the right to remind you what you will need to take.

Tracksuit

Training shoes to warm up in

Competition shoes (spikes, road shoes or cross-country shoes)

Spare laces

Replacement spikes and spike key

Shorts and vest (in your club colours)

Socks and underwear

Rain suit if it is wet

Running tights, gloves etc if it is cold

Sweatbands if it is hot

Race number (if you have it)

Safety pins

Towel

Soap and shampoo

Comb

Stopwatch

Plasters

Drink and food for after the race

★ If you already have your race number, pin it to your vest. You do not want to be fiddling around with safety pins just before the race.

★ Check your shoes – replace any broken spikes or frayed laces.

★ Don't train frantically the day before. It is too late to gain any benefit from training, and you will only tire yourself. Save your energy for the race.

★ Avoid experimenting with new or unusual meals the day before a race in case they upset your stomach. It is best to stick to foods you know agree with you.

★ Make sure you get a good night's sleep. Avoid parties, discos and nights out on the day before a competition.

The morning of the race

★ Plan your day carefully, allowing plenty of time for each thing you have to do. Last minute panics cost energy, and may upset your mental preparation for the race.

★ Set out for the competition in good time. It is better to arrive early than to be rushed. Make sure you know where the competition is and how to get there.

★ Do not eat anything in the last two or three hours before the competition, to give you time to digest the food. Keep to simple foods that are easy to digest, such as toast or cereals.

★ Avoid fizzy drinks, tea and coffee during the period before a race. Drink water or fresh fruit juice instead.

When you arrive at the competition

★ Report to the race officials.

★ Check all the arrangements, so that you know what to do and where to go. Pay attention to what is going on – sometimes there are last minute changes to the competition programme.

★ Change into your race kit.

★ Plan your warm-up carefully, so that you complete it just prior to the start of your event.

★ If possible, look at the list of competitors to see who has been drawn in your heat. You may want to modify your race plan once you know who your opponents are.

★ Keep warm and relaxed until you are called to the start.

★ If a problem arises, stay calm and find someone (such as a coach or an official) who can help you to sort it out.

During the race

★ Be determined and single-minded.

★ Concentrate on giving your best performance.

★ Don't be distracted by the other competitors. As far as possible, stick to your race plan.

★ In cross-country and road races, make sure you follow any instructions from the officials at the finish. Go right down any finishing chutes, so that the officials can see that you have completed the race.

After the competition

★ Put on your track suit.

★ Go through your warming-down exercises (see pages 36-37).

★ Review your performance and how well your tactics worked. Learn from any mistakes you made, so that you do not repeat them next time. But be positive – learn from the things you did well, too.

★ If the opportunity arises, thank the officials. Most are volunteers who receive little thanks for giving up their free time.

Mental preparation

As well as preparing physically for your race, it is a good idea to try to get yourself into a confident and positive frame of mind. If you start the race expecting to lose, you are not likely to win. Many top athletes use techniques like the ones below to help them approach important races with a winning attitude.

★ Set yourself realistic aims. Achieving small goals, such as completing a fun run or improving your personal best time, will boost your confidence.

★ Don't waste time worrying about all the things that could go wrong during the race. Instead, practise thinking positively. Visualize yourself running well and achieving a good finishing position. Imagine the sense of fulfilment as you pass the finish line.

★ Go through your tactics mentally several times before the race starts. Rehearse your pace, how you will cope with any difficult parts of the course and how you will deal with tiredness.

★ If you often get very nervous before the start, organize a warm-up routine and rehearse it both physically and in your head so that it becomes automatic. On race day, going through the familiar routine will help to calm you down.

★ If you do get butterflies, remember that this is your body's way of preparing for the race. Try not to let them make you tense up, and they will help, not hinder you. Once you start running, the adrenalin in your body which causes this feeling will enable you to give your best performance.

Running injuries

Running injuries are unfortunately very common. The continuous pounding of running puts stress on your feet and legs, which can lead to injuries if you do not have a balanced training programme and a good technique. It is also possible to injure yourself by falling or by over-stretching. You can read about some common injuries below.

Most injuries require expert medical attention, especially if the symptoms persist for more than a few days. Do not try to treat anything other than minor cuts and bruises yourself.

Blisters

Blisters are caused by friction, for example from a seam on a sock or shoe rubbing against your skin. They can often be prevented by wearing thick, seamless socks, or by putting talcum powder in your shoes to keep your feet dry.

If you do get a blister, you should puncture it with a needle. Sterilize the needle first by passing it through a flame (such as a match). Pierce the blister on two sides, and press the fluid out with a clean tissue or a piece of cotton wool. Do not remove the top of the blister.

Cramp

This is a sudden pain in a limb due to the contraction of a group of muscles. It may be caused by lactic acid building up in your muscles during exercise (see page 7). It can also be due to dehydration, so if you are prone to cramp make sure you drink plenty of water both before and after running.

If you do develop cramp in your leg or foot, it can be relieved by straightening the cramped area. Ask someone else to do this for you, as shown below.

Stitch

This is a sharp, nagging pain beneath your rib cage which often starts in the middle of a run. No-one is sure what causes it, but it is often triggered by running too soon after a meal. Always wait at least two or three hours after eating before setting out on your run.

Stitch may also be caused by working your diaphragm muscle too hard. This is most common in unfit runners. If you do develop a stitch while running, you may find it helps to slow down and bend forwards, as this relaxes the diaphragm.

Cramp in the foot

Ask someone to straighten your toes by pushing them upwards, then stand on the ball of your foot.

Cramp in the calf

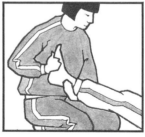

Ask someone to straighten your knee, and then pull your foot up towards your shin as shown above.

Cramp in the thigh

Ask someone to straighten your knee, pull your leg up and forwards, then gently press your knee down.

Osgood-Schlatter's disease

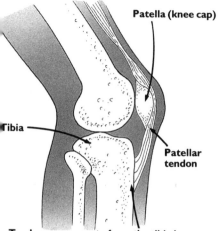

Patella (knee cap)

Tibia

Patellar tendon

Tendon can separate from the tibia here.

This is a knee problem which is very common in teenagers. The main symptom is pain below the knee which is brought on by any vigorous movement, such as jumping, landing or kicking. It is caused by the patellar tendon separating slightly from the tibia (see diagram above).

This problem is thought to be brought on by over-use of the knee, and treatment usually consists of complete rest for at least six weeks. If the problem persists, you may have to give up running, at least until your bones have finished growing.

Pulled muscles

Muscles and tendons can be pulled or torn by any awkward movement, such as twisting your ankle or tripping over. It is very common for runners to pull muscles in their legs.

The best first aid for a pulled muscle is an ice pack (see right), which relieves the pain and swelling. It may also help to elevate the limb (by sitting with your foot up on a sofa, for example), as this ensures that any excess blood in the area will be recirculated in the body. If the muscle is extremely painful you must consult a doctor.

When you restart training, strapping or an elasticated bandage may help to prevent further twisting of the muscle.

Making an ice pack

An ice pack is useful for treating many common sports injuries, such as bruises, sprains and pulled muscles. Use one as soon as possible after the injury. An ice pack reduces swelling, as the cold forces blood out of the area. When the pack is removed, fresh blood flows into the area and speeds the healing process.

You can make an ice pack at home with some ice cubes from the fridge. Put them in a plastic bag and wrap this in a cloth or thin towel. Never put ice directly on to your skin as it can give you an ice burn. Hold the ice pack on the injury for about ten minutes.

Avoiding injury

Many injuries can be avoided if you take simple precautions such as the ones below.

★ Always warm up and down properly (see pages 36-37). It is much easier to tear or strain a cold muscle.

★ Wear proper running shoes that protect your feet well.

★ Don't run further than the recommended distances for your age. Many injuries are caused by working your muscles and tendons too hard.

★ Stop if you feel pain – this is a signal that something is wrong. Consult your doctor.

★ Run on soft surfaces such as grass whenever possible, as this puts much less stress on your joints than road running.

★ Make sure your training includes stretching and strengthening exercises.

★ Don't rush your training – aim to progress slowly.

★ Take an easy or rest day after a hard day's training.

Index